This is a fictionalised biography describing some
of the key moments (so far!) in the career of
Raheem Sterling.
Some of the events described in this book are
based upon the author's imagination and are
probably not entirely accurate representations
of what actually happened.

Tales from the Pitch
Sterling
by Harry Coninx

Published in the United State of American and Canada
by Leapfrog Press
www.leapfrogpress.com

ISBN: 978-1-948585-90-3
First published in 2024

Distributed in the United States by
Consortium Book Sales and Distribution
St Paul, Minnesota, 55114
www.cbsd.com

First published in the United Kingdom (2023 second edition 2024)
by Raven Books
An imprint of Ransom Publishing Ltd.
Unit 7, Brocklands Farm, West Meon, Hampshire GU32 1JN, UK
www.ransom.co.uk

TALES FROM THE PITCH

RAHEEM STERLING

HARRY CONINX

Leapfrog Press
New York and London

For my mum, who has put up with a lot of years of Hall Football

CONTENTS

I

THE TREBLE

May 2019, Wembley Stadium, London, England
FA Cup Final, Man City v Watford

"I broke a window down that street!" Raheem shouted to anyone who might be listening, "Playing football."

The Man City bus was winding its way through the neighbourhood Raheem had grown up in, and he had his face pressed up against the window so he could watch the familiar sights as they rolled past.

"And one round the corner from here!" he yelled again.

"It's a good thing your shooting has got better since those days," Sergio Agüero laughed next to him, "or we wouldn't be in the final!"

A ripple of laughter ran through the bus. The Man City team were focused but relaxed. They were on course for the domestic treble and a win today, against Watford, would seal the deal.

Today was FA Cup Final day.

Despite being heavy favourites, City couldn't afford to take Watford for granted. Watford were a mid-table side, for sure, but clearly they had what was needed to get to the final. They weren't a team to be underestimated.

Raheem listened intently as Pep Guardiola, the Man City manager, spoke to the players.

"Right, lads, today is Vinnie's last game," he said, gesturing to their captain Vincent Kompany. "So let's send him out with a bang and bring back our third trophy of the season!"

The bus jolted to a halt. They had arrived at their destination: Wembley Stadium. It was the home of English football and Raheem could remember, as an awestruck child, watching the stadium being constructed.

No matter how many times he played here his heart always swelled with pride at what he'd achieved. As a young boy, growing up just down the road from the stadium, he'd always dreamed of playing at Wembley. Now it was a reality.

In the tunnel, the City players were brimming with confidence. Raheem even heard a few laughs coming from the back of their line.

He glanced to his right at the Watford players. They stood in complete silence, with nervousness evident on each player's face.

"I don't think they're up for it, man," Raheem whispered to Gabriel Jesus in front of him.

Out on the pitch, Raheem couldn't tear his eyes away from the sea of sky blue in their half of the stadium. City's loyal fans had turned up in huge numbers.

As well as being the cup final, this was also the last game of the season before the summer break, and there was definitely a party atmosphere amongst the City fans. To many of them it was as if the cup was already won.

Dangerous thinking, thought Raheem.

Indeed, within 20 minutes City's hopes were almost ended.

Watford's Gerard Deulofeu had burst away down the right-hand side and squared it to Roberto Pereyra. He was in on goal and, for a brief moment, Raheem thought he had been wrong in what he'd said in the tunnel about Watford.

But City keeper Ederson burst forward and smothered the ball, allowing Kyle Walker to sprint across and clear it.

Raheem took a sharp breath. If City needed a wake-up call in this game, that had been it.

"Wake up now, boys!" Kevin de Bruyne yelled, as City recovered the ball.

Raheem responded and soon had the ball, spinning away from the Watford players surrounding him. He saw

David Silva to his left, but decided to ignore him. The goal was beckoning in the distance and they needed the lead. He was up for this.

Then several of the Watford defenders clattered into him, desperately throwing themselves in front of the ball. Raheem watched as the ball spun up into the air and fell back to the ground.

David pulled it down and sent it back towards him. The Watford defenders were still on the floor as Raheem jumped to meet the ball.

He flicked it back towards David with a neat header. It was perfectly judged – David brought it down and smashed it past the Watford keeper.

GOAL!

City had the lead.

"That must be the first time you've ever won a header, Raheem!" David bellowed, as they celebrated in front of the screaming City fans. The deafening noise was like music to Raheem's ears.

"That's one hand on the trophy, boys!" Vincent shouted.

But the goal hadn't quite killed off Watford, and

Raheem knew all too well that no game was won with just a one-goal lead. They needed another.

And Bernardo Silva made it happen.

Bernardo lofted the ball into the box and it came to Gabriel Jesus at the back post. He poked it over the goalkeeper and, as it bounced, Raheem instinctively sprinted in, smashing it over the line.

GOAL! 2-0.

"That's *my* goal, Raheem!" Gabriel shouted, as Raheem celebrated. "Don't you *dare* steal that!"

"Just had to make sure, pal. You can never be too careful," Raheem laughed back, hugging his team-mate.

At half-time City were still 2-0 up and Raheem was savouring every moment with his team.

"Good goal, Gabi!" Pep roared as they walked into the dressing room.

"What? That was mine, wasn't it?" Raheem yelled, jokingly raising his arms in protest.

"I spoke to the ref – he says it's Gabi's goal," Pep chuckled.

"Ha! Told you!" Gabi laughed, as he gently punched Raheem on the arm.

The team's spirits remained sky-high and City kept up the pressure after the restart. Within twenty minutes Kevin and Gabi had made it 4-0.

"That one's definitely mine!" Gabi shouted at Raheem, as they celebrated his goal. Raheem just laughed. He was feeling too giddy to fire any banter back.

The game – and the cup – was surely in the bag.

With their team now four down, the stadium began to empty of Watford fans. All that could be heard was the deafening noise of the City faithful. They had travelled all this way from Manchester for their team, and thousands more were outside the stadium, waiting for the now inevitable celebrations.

Raheem wanted to give the fans something more, and he saw his chance with only ten minutes left on the clock.

Bernardo had burst down the left-hand side and fizzed the ball across. Raheem sprinted into the box and smashed it high into the roof of the net.

GOAL!

He sprinted towards the fans and held up three

fingers. The crowd went mad, knowing exactly what it meant – it was for the three trophies that City had now won this season.

Spurred on by the noise, Raheem soon found himself taking another shot after De Bruyne had fired the ball into the box.

The ball cannoned off the post and came back towards Raheem's feet. He instantly knew there was only one place it was going.

GOAL!

Minutes later, the final whistle blew and Watford were finally put out of their misery.

The final score was 6-0 to Man City. Raheem had scored two goals in an FA Cup victory! He held his hands to his face in awe and disbelief.

City had made history – and he was at the centre of it. The first team ever to do the domestic treble of the Premier League, the League Cup and the FA Cup. And finishing it off in style with a historic 6-0 win.

Raheem celebrated with the team – his friends – as cannons fired confetti and Vincent held the trophy high in the air.

It had been a whirlwind journey to get here but, as Raheem looked out at the roaring fans, the twenty-four-year-old felt no signs of slowing down yet.

2

WEMBLEY ONE DAY

March 2005,
Vernon House special school, London

Raheem peered nervously around the door, looking into the classroom.

His teacher, Mr Beschi, was sitting at the desk at the front of the room, tapping his fingers on the wooden top.

Raheem had really warmed to Mr Beschi, which was something new. He'd not had good relationships with any of the teachers in his last primary school. But Raheem just felt that this teacher really understood him.

Which is why the thought that he'd been ordered in, with his mum, for a meeting with Mr Beschi seemed to make no sense.

As if on cue, Nadine Sterling marched past her son and headed straight into the room.

Mr Beschi stood up and the two exchanged greetings, while Raheem sat himself down quietly next to them, desperately trying to remember what he might have done wrong that would have landed him here.

He really didn't want to disappoint his mum. She'd moved their family from Jamaica to England to give them a better life and, even though his memories of his earlier years were a bit fuzzy, he could remember how hard it had been for her.

Raheem was well aware that he'd already been adding to his mum's stresses by playing up at his last primary school. He'd hoped he was through all that now – he really didn't want to make things worse for his mum all over again.

Mr Beschi noticed Raheem's concerned expression.

"No need to look so worried, Raheem", Mr Beschi said soothingly. "We're just keeping your mum in the loop."

Mr Beschi had always been fond of Raheem. From that very first day, when this small boy had shyly walked into his class, he could sense that Raheem was one of those good kids that trouble somehow just seemed to follow around.

Mr Beschi turned back to Nadine and started to fill her in on her son's progress. Raheem was trying hard, he told her, and seemed to be responding well to the small size of the class.

But he was still easily influenced by others in the class and all too often he ended up behaving badly, even though he knew it was wrong.

As soon as Raheem realised he wasn't in trouble, he switched off. He didn't need to listen any more. It was a Friday, and his mates would all be playing football in the park. That was where he wanted to be.

"What do you enjoy most about school at the moment, Raheem?" his teacher asked gently, bringing him back into the room.

Raheem looked up and smiled. It was an easy question to answer.

"Football. We smashed you today." Raheem's face had now cracked into a wicked grin.

Mr Beschi chuckled. Every day, the staff played five-a-side with the kids, and it was common knowledge that having Raheem on your side was better than having an extra adult.

In today's game, Raheem had run rings around Mr Beschi and they both knew it. Raheem hadn't stopped grinning – he seemed to find it hilarious how much better he was than everyone else.

"Well, you definitely have a talent beyond your years for football," Mr Beschi said, before pausing. "You know, it's all in your hands, Raheem. I've told you this before. You just need to make the right choices, eh?"

The meeting drew to a close and, as Raheem left the room with his mum, he turned and gave his teacher a little nod.

Mr Beschi gave simple advice, and Raheem liked that. He also had the feeling that Mr Beschi was genuinely rooting for him, and that felt good too.

Beyond his immediate family, Raheem wasn't sure he'd ever had that feeling of support before.

"I can guess where you want to go now, and I bet it isn't to do your homework," his mum said, as they walked out the school's front doors.

Raheem quickly explained that playing football technically *was* homework – it was homework for his training at Queens Park Rangers tomorrow.

As they continued along the street he was soon babbling on about how his coach had told him that he was going to be a star.

"That's what your grandma said when you were a toddler on the beaches, kicking sand at everyone," Nadine laughed.

Raheem couldn't remember doing that, but he smiled proudly anyway.

"I told your gran, No. He's going to be a doctor or a lawyer," his mum continued. "A job where he can support his mother when she's all old," she teased, bumping shoulders with Raheem.

"Do you know how much footballers get paid, mum?" he laughed back. "I'll buy you *ten* houses when I'm a footballer. With … "

He paused, trying to think of something he could buy for his mum that would do her justice, that would repay her support and love for him. He'd never really thought about what a top footballer's wage could buy you; he just wanted to kick a ball around, all day, every day.

" … with diamond sinks in it!" he finished.

They both looked at each other and started laughing at his ridiculous suggestion, but their joking was cut short as they turned the next corner.

In the distance, towering over the rows of houses, they could see a mass of cranes leaning over a huge construction site.

"I'm going to be playing there one day, Mum," Raheem said, as he stared longingly at what was going to be the new Wembley Stadium.

Nadine could sense the change in her son's tone.

"I know you will," she said gently.

The pair kept walking until the boys he'd befriended on the estate came into view at the entrance to the local park. They were already tapping a ball around and Raheem instantly picked up his pace so he could get involved.

As he and his mum parted ways, Nadine promised him she'd be back in exactly two hours to pick him up.

She didn't want him walking home alone in the dark in *this* neighbourhood.

3

THE RIGHT CHOICE

February 2010, QPR training ground, London

Scouts were scattered along the sideline for QPR's reserve game, their hands shoved deep into their pockets to shield them from the cold winter air.

Raheem looked at them with determination.

He knew that most of his footballing heroes had already been at their clubs by the time they were fifteen. Yet here he was, fifteen himself, still at QPR and not even in their first team. It was frustrating. This wasn't how it was supposed to be.

"You shouldn't worry, Raheem," his coach, Benny, had said to him when he'd voiced his frustration a few weeks ago. "Most players don't make their debuts till they're eighteen or nineteen."

"I don't want to be 'most players' though," Raheem had muttered back. "I want to be better. I want to be the best."

Now, as he stepped on to the pitch, he felt a shiver of excitement at the thought that this could be the match that would seal the first deal of his career.

But as soon as the game kicked off, Raheem forgot all about the scouts. He was just too busy enjoying playing football.

Nevertheless, he put on a dominant performance right from the start. Raheem used to hate being so small for his age, but he soon realised that in football it had its advantages.

Being small made him quick and nimble, and in this game, as in most games, the opposition players struggled to get close to him.

Even when they did get close, they almost always ended up fouling him and sending him flying to the ground.

At one point in the game Raheem flinched, trying to dodge a challenge that didn't come in, and then he fell over a leg that wasn't there.

"Dive! Cheat!" the opposition players shouted, as they surrounded the ref, furious with Raheem.

Raheem tried to make them understand that he wasn't trying to cheat – he'd just thought a challenge was coming in. But his appeal fell on deaf ears.

The game got back underway and the players continued to kick him, now even more than before.

After the match, Raheem marched straight over to Benny.

"They were kicking me all game! I just thought he was going to do it again, and I didn't want a broken ankle or something!"

Benny nodded understandingly. He'd spotted Raheem's talent right from his very first week at QPR, and had taken him under his wing to try and keep him on the straight and narrow.

Raheem's unstoppable energy sometimes made Benny feel as if that was an impossible job, but he'd never given up on trying to rein him in.

"I know it's tough, Raheem, but even if you've been kicked all afternoon, you can't just have a go back at them."

With his little lecture over, Benny was keen to change the subject. "Listen, Raheem, I've got someone who's excited to meet you … "

Raheem nodded, still slightly bitter at being cast as the bad guy of the match. He trudged behind Benny, who led him to a man who instantly held out a hand to him.

"Hello there. You must be Raheem."

"Yeah?" Raheem replied cautiously, shaking the man's hand.

"I work with Liverpool. I thought you might like to know that Rafa wants to bring you in."

"Rafa Benítez?" Sterling said, astonished. "He's seen me play?"

"He has, Raheem," Benny chimed in. In fact, Liverpool have made an offer for you."

Raheem's mouth dropped open. He stared blankly at the two men, looking from one to the other, trying to take it in.

Liverpool, one of the biggest clubs in Europe, were taking a chance on him.

"I didn't want to tell you before the match and throw you off," the Liverpool scout said with a chuckle.

Raheem barely heard him. A hundred thoughts and questions flashed through his mind. But before he could let himself get carried away by the incredible thought of pulling on a red shirt, he had one big thing to do. He had to ask his mum.

Raheem couldn't get home fast enough, and he spent the whole journey thinking of ways to try to get her onside with the move. The key, he decided, would be breaking the news to her gently.

But when he got home, he knew instantly that the club had beaten him to it. His mum looked completely furious.

"Before you say anything," Raheem prattled,

"I really think I should do this. It's going to be so good for my career. Liverpool have had so many young players and … "

His mum held her hand up, cutting him off. Straight away, Raheem stopped talking.

She'd already said "No" when clubs like Arsenal, Chelsea, and Fulham had enquired after him, and it was looking as if this offer would go the same way.

"I think you should do it."

"Wha … ?" Raheem said, completely shocked. "Why?"

"Because I think Liverpool will be a good place for you."

Nadine had long been anxious about the part of London they lived in, and how it was having a negative impact on her impressionable son. They lived on a tough estate and she was desperate to prevent Raheem from being led astray.

Letting him go to Liverpool was an opportunity to do just that.

Raheem crossed the tiny kitchen and gave his mum a massive hug.

He didn't need to tell her how much he was going to miss her – she knew that already.

So he just whispered in her ear. "I think it's the right choice."

4

GOING NORTH

September 2010, Liverpool training ground, Liverpool

Raheem's seven months at Liverpool had been the best time ever.

It hadn't felt as if it was going to be that way after his first night in the city. He'd lain in his bed and struggled for hours to get to sleep, because the mattress didn't feel like his mattress at home.

Other worries had kept him awake as well. Who

would he stand with in training? Would he make new friends? Would he get on with the others in the squad? Would he be *good enough*?

His football skills had made him something of a celebrity on his estate back home and he was so used to just knowing everyone. Now things were going to be very different.

But all of that had melted away as soon as he'd stepped out on to the Liverpool training ground and had the ball at his feet.

He was too focused on soaking up every bit of advice he was being given by the coaches to worry about little details. After all, these coaches were the best – they knew their stuff and their job was to teach *him*. *His* job was to suck it all in. It was a no-brainer.

And on top of that, regularly rubbing shoulders with superstars like Dirk Kuyt, Fernando Torres and Jamie Carragher was massive.

He remembered the first time Steven Gerrard had spoken to him.

"You're Raheem, right?" Stevie had said, sticking his hand out in greeting. Raheem had reached out and shaken his hand, completely star-struck by the legend standing in front of him. He could feel himself actually shaking.

"Rafa reckons you're going to be a star," Stevie continued, with a friendly smile.

Raheem nodded, not at all sure what to say. "Well, I hope I can reach your expectations," he finally mumbled, immediately kicking himself for saying something so lame.

"I'm sure you will," Stevie had replied, before strolling away.

Luckily, embarrassing moments like that had been rare, as Raheem had spent his seven months training with the reserves. He liked all the lads and was always excited to train with them, but today he could feel a different buzz in the air.

Rafa had been replaced over the summer by Roy Hodgson, from Fulham, and there were rumours that a lot of the big players didn't like the new manager.

"I heard that he's going to try and sell Torres," Conor Coady muttered to Raheem, as they jogged across the training pitch.

"No way, man!" Suso shouted across from the other side, overhearing the conversation. "I heard that he's going to drop Gerrard and Carragher."

"Well, that's fine by me! He might put us in the first team, then!" Raheem responded.

Getting into the first team was all Raheem could think about, even if it did mean risking embarrassing himself in front of Stevie again.

The other players gave him a look.

"He hasn't even come down and spoken to us yet, Raheem," Suso said. "Why would he call us up to the first team?"

Raheem shrugged. He was still hoping that they might get an opportunity.

He was wrong. They didn't get a call up to the main team and within three months Roy had been sacked. Kenny Dalglish, a former Liverpool legend, was brought in as his replacement, and he actually did come and speak to the younger players.

"You guys are going to be my future stars, alright?" Kenny said in his thick Scottish accent.

Raheem looked around at his friends, Jonjo Shelvey,

Jay Spearing and Martin Kelly, to see what they were making of this. They all looked nervous.

"You'll all get opportunities in the first team over the next year. And when you get that opportunity, I want you to take it and impress me," Kenny finished, glaring intensely around the room.

Raheem nodded. That made perfect sense to him. He could see the other lads feeling the pressure of Kenny's words, but for him it was exactly what he wanted. He'd already been fighting to be seen at every opportunity – it actually felt good to know that now somebody would be watching.

In the next reserve game against Southend, Raheem scored five goals. Each one was better than the last.

"If that's not impressive, then I don't know what is," Raheem said breathlessly to Conor after the game.

"You could have scored six, to be fair," Conor chuckled.

5

LUIS'S WAY

March 2012, Liverpool Training Ground, Liverpool

Luis Suárez played football in a completely different way from anyone Raheem had ever played with before.

The superstar had been brought to Liverpool by Kenny Dalglish, and he fascinated Raheem.

On one occasion, during a rare opportunity to train with the first team, Raheem had failed to pass the ball to Luis when he was one-on-one. Instead, he'd gone for a shot. It had been a poor effort and had gone well wide of the goal.

"What was that?"

Raheem heard the angry shout from the other side of the pitch. Luis had his arms outstretched and a furious glare on his face.

"Pass me the ball!" he screamed again, slapping his hands together in complete frustration. "Rubbish!"

Raheem had never seen anyone take training so seriously, and he was completely captivated by Luis's passion. Only minutes later, Luis was flying into a challenge with Jordan Henderson, almost taking his leg off.

"Luis, calm it down, man," Gerrard shouted, and a lot of the other players nodded in agreement.

But Raheem loved the way that Luis played every moment of his football with the same urgency and passion.

"Why do you play like that all the time?" he'd timidly asked him during a short break from the session.

Luis laughed.

"Where I come from, football is all or nothing," he

said. "If I hadn't have become a footballer, I would have been a nothing, a nobody," he continued. "So I have to play every minute the same, because I worked so hard to be here. It's either everything, or it's nothing."

Raheem nodded. He didn't really know much about Uruguay, Luis's country, but he understood what he was saying.

In the same kind of way, Raheem didn't know what he'd be doing without football. If he was honest with himself, he knew that if it wasn't for football he'd probably never have made it off his estate.

The pair chatted for a while, before Luis turned and sprinted back into training. All Raheem could think was that he was glad the guy was on his team, and that he wasn't up against him.

Training alongside superstars such as Luis was certainly teaching Raheem a lot, and his improved skills had attracted Kenny's attention.

With an FA Cup final looming, Kenny was looking to rest some of Liverpool's bigger names. Some, like

Luis, refused to be rested, but several others were happy for the break, so Kenny was looking to the reserve options.

When Raheem heard he had been named on the bench for the first time, in a match against Wigan Athletic, he was beside himself.

This debut was what he'd been working for from the moment he'd stepped through the door at Liverpool. After all, playing Premier League football was what it was all about.

"Now Raheem, you might not get on the pitch," Kenny warned him before the match, "but it will be good for you to experience a match day."

"Yes, boss," Raheem replied eagerly. Needless to say, he had every hope that he'd get the chance to go on.

The game got off to a shaky start. Wigan were fired up and the Liverpool players seemed to be somewhere else altogether.

Raheem watched from the dugout as the team made mistake after mistake.

After a while he turned to Jonjo Shelvey, sitting next

to him on the bench. "What's going on, man? Why are we playing like this?"

Jonjo shrugged.

Minutes later and Liverpool's woes went from bad to worse after a clumsy challenge by Martin Škrtel on Wigan attacker Victor Moses.

The referee immediately pointed to the penalty spot as groans echoed around Anfield. Raheem looked at Kenny Dalglish, who had his head in his hands.

The penalty was converted and Liverpool were on course for their fifth defeat in six straight games.

Kenny was a club legend, so he'd been given a decent amount of time to try and turn things around at the club. But the fans were running out of patience and some booing could be heard in the far corners of the stadium.

The atmosphere in the dressing room at half-time was quiet and tense. None of the younger players said a word, casting anxious glances amongst themselves as Kenny shouted at his team.

"I'm glad that's not aimed at us," Raheem whispered to Jonjo, who solemnly nodded back.

But Kenny's harsh words seemed to inspire Liverpool,

as minutes into the second half Steven Gerrard combined with Luis Suárez, who slotted Liverpool level on terms.

"Come on!" Raheem shouted, punching his fist in the air for Luis. He was such a force out there – it was just what Raheem wanted to be.

Raheem had thought that Liverpool would push on once they'd levelled the scores, but fifteen minutes later Wigan were back in front and Jonjo was summoned from his seat next to Raheem.

Ten minutes later, Raheem was also called on. He was ready in seconds, desperate not to give Kenny any reason to change his mind.

"Right, Raheem, just give it your best shot," the manager grunted. "I'm not expecting too much from you on your first outing."

With that he shoved Raheem out on to the Anfield turf.

Adrenaline rushed through Raheem's body at the feeling of being out on the pitch, and he wanted to celebrate each and every touch he got. Then, in what felt like no time at all, it was over.

He'd loved every second out there, but he wanted to have done more to impress his manager.

He thought he might try and talk to Kenny after the game, but the manager was long gone.

Raheem sensed that Kenny Dalglish had far more important things on his mind.

6
IT'S A START

August 2012, Anfield Stadium, Liverpool
Liverpool v Man City

"I hope we get Mourinho or someone like that," Jonjo said excitedly, when the talk of Kenny's exit was rife.

"I hope we don't," Raheem replied, "he never plays young players."

It wasn't long before there was a change of manager at the club, and Raheem's wish for a coach who would play younger players seemed to have been answered.

Kenny had been replaced by Brendan Rogers.

Even though new managers always brought upheaval, Raheem was excited. He knew that change was worth it if it got him in with a chance of playing more than ten minutes every now and then.

And here he was, starting against Man City of all teams.

This was even more of a shock considering what had happened a few weeks ago, when he'd been subbed on in a game against the Hungarian side FC Gomel.

Raheem had been terrorising the Gomel defence for most of the game, despite being repeatedly fouled by them. Every time he'd hit the ground, the crowd would look on anxiously, fearing the worst for the slight teenager.

They hadn't realised that Raheem was very used to being brought down, and were amazed that each time he'd just jump back up on his feet, smile at his larger opponents and then beat them at the very next opportunity.

Everything in the game had seemed to be going very smoothly – Raheem had played well and they'd run out

1-0 winners. But then at full-time, back in the dressing room, Rogers had torn into the side.

"That was really awful!" he raged. "I expect to see you all in training bright and early tomorrow."

Raheem had then raised an eyebrow at Jordan Henderson, sitting opposite him. He just felt it was a bit harsh, seeing that they'd won the game.

"Don't you raise your eyebrows when I'm talking, son!" Brendan had suddenly hissed, gesturing at Raheem.

"Sorry, boss," Raheem had muttered, feeling completely embarrassed at being spotted.

He'd kept his head down for the rest of Brendan's speech, not wanting to cause a further scene. It felt like being back in school, accidentally being at the centre of trouble and being hated by the teacher.

It didn't leave Raheem with a warm feeling.

But evidently Brendan didn't completely hate him. In fact, starting him in such a high-profile game against Man City suggested that he trusted Raheem.

Either way, Raheem wanted to repair things with his manager. Otherwise, he knew it would be his football that suffered. He had to play well today.

"It looks as though they're going to play a back three, so you're going to have an opportunity to really get at some of their centre-backs," Rodgers had said to him before the game.

As he walked out on to the pitch, Raheem focused on what Rodgers had told him, rather than letting himself be distracted by thinking about the array of superstars he was up against today.

He began the game at a pace he didn't even know he could play at. The City players knew what to expect from Suárez and Gerrard, but they hadn't played against this Sterling guy before.

The City centre-backs Kolo Touré and Pablo Zabaleta couldn't get anywhere close to him, and when they did, they couldn't get anywhere near the ball.

Just minutes in, Raheem fired a ball across the face of goal, which their new player, Borini, really should have tapped in. Borini was quickly on the receiving end of a rant from Luis Suárez.

"He does that, man," Raheem said to Borini. "Don't worry about it."

The game was end-to-end and ultimately finished in a 2-2 draw. As the whistle blew, Raheem realised that he'd actually stayed on the pitch for the full 90 minutes and he was elated.

"Raheem, that was sensational!" Brendan Rodgers shouted, coming over to him at full time.

Raheem breathed a sigh of relief. Too often in his life people had taken a dislike to him that he couldn't seem to shift. So it was good to hear he'd managed to get Brendan at least partly back on side.

"Well done, Raheem." He heard a thick South American accent behind him. He turned and beamed at Luis, knowing that the Uruguayan didn't give praise easily.

But he knew there was one thing he really needed to do to get Luis's full respect. He needed to score. He'd already got a goal for the senior team in a friendly against Bayer Leverkusen, but now he wanted one that really counted.

7

IT'S A GOAL!

October 2012, Anfield Stadium, Liverpool
Liverpool v Reading

"Score." It was the only word Raheem allowed himself to think about as he stepped onto the pitch for the match against Reading.

He had put in some solid performances and by now had firmly established himself in the first team. He had been quickly joined by Suso.

"Can you believe it?" Raheem had shouted excitedly

to Suso, when they'd seen the team list for today. "Me and you in the Liverpool first team? It's insane!"

The game was quickly underway and the pair were playing behind Luis Suárez, carefully following his example.

Raheem was continually on the alert, ready for any chance to make what he'd come to do happen.

Then, with half an hour gone, a flick from Luis put Raheem in. His pace took him away from the Reading defenders and he burst into the box.

This was the moment he'd been tirelessly working for. Raheem swung at the ball, but scuffed it slightly and it bobbled away along the ground. The noise of the Anfield ground subsided and it felt like everything went quiet.

The bobble was working in his favour, though. A tricky bounce took the ball over the goalkeeper, before settling in the back of the net.

GOAL!

Raheem almost didn't know what to do. He looked to the sky, then looked to his team-mates, before sprinting towards the fans.

He slid on the turf and collapsed to the ground as Luis tackled him. They were soon joined by the rest of the team, who all piled on top of Raheem, ecstatic for him.

It was the biggest moment of his career so far.

The game finished in a 1-0 win for Liverpool, meaning that it was Raheem's goal that had won them the game. A goal is always a goal, but not every goal is a match winner.

"What a moment, Raheem!" Gerrard shouted to him as they went off at full-time. "I remember my first goal for Liverpool, just like it was yesterday. You never forget it."

Raheem beamed at the idea of being like Gerrard one day, with all those goals under his belt, but still being able to remember his very first one.

He called his mum as soon as he was out of the ground.

"Mum, Mum, did you see?" he babbled down the line. "What did you think?"

"Of course I saw, Raheem," she replied. "I got

everyone back here to watch it. Lakima, Kimberley, Kingston, Nana … "

As his mum reeled off the names of those in his family, he wished he could be with them to celebrate this special moment.

"You must be the youngest goal scorer for Liverpool ever," his mum continued.

"Stevie was telling me that Michael Owen was younger, so no, not quite. But there's plenty more records I'm going to get!"

8
THREE LIONS

October 2012, Liverpool training ground, Liverpool

Raheem knew that the call was coming, so he'd kept his phone close all day, checking it regularly. But when it finally did ring, his heart still skipped a beat.

"Hello, Mr Hodgson," he spluttered, knowing exactly who the unidentified caller was.

It was Brendan who had tipped him off that the new England manager, Roy Hodgson, had been in touch.

Raheem's relationship with the Liverpool manager still had a bit of an edge to it at times, but certainly this time Brendan seemed genuinely happy for him.

The news shouldn't have been a surprise. Raheem was now an important part of the side and had formed a good partnership with Suárez in the Liverpool attack. They were getting good results for their team.

And of course Raheem had some knowledge of Roy from their short time together at Liverpool.

"Hi, Raheem," Roy said slowly down the line. "I'm sure you've heard I want to try out a few younger players in my next England squad, to get them used to playing for the national team."

The words 'England squad' were running round and round in Raheem's head. It felt like a daydream.

"And that means me?" Raheem pressed. He had to be sure he had this right, because it felt too good to be true.

"Yeah, son. I want you to see if you have future in this team," Roy replied.

Raheem had already stepped up for England's under-21 team, but this was different.

This was the big league, the real deal.

Yet, after waiting all day for this call, Raheem was struggling to know what to say in reply.

"It would be an honour," he said quickly. And he meant it.

Having been born in Jamaica, Raheem had the option to play for either the Jamaican national side or for England. But England had always been his home, and having grown up so close to the iconic Wembley Stadium, it really was a no-brainer.

He put the phone down next to him and stared at the clock. Getting out on to the pitch and playing for his country couldn't come quickly enough.

Just a month later, Raheem was standing in the players' tunnel at the Friends Arena in Stockholm. His first appearance for England, this was a friendly against Sweden.

As he waited to run out on to the pitch, he couldn't stop looking down at the three lions on his shirt. He imagined his mum watching at home, and his other friends from the estate, friends that he'd now lost touch with, and …

It occurred to him there was one other person who had always said that he would play for England one day – his teacher, Mr Beschi.

And now, at seventeen, here he was, starting for England.

He began to follow his team-mates onto the pitch, desperately hoping that his old teacher was watching the game on TV.

It was a back and forth game, and after Zlatan Ibrahimović put the Swedes in front, Steven Caulker managed to scramble England back on level terms. It was a goal on his debut and a huge moment for the centre back. Raheem couldn't help but feel a little bit jealous.

When Danny Welbeck then managed to get England 2-1 ahead, it looked as if they were on course for a comfortable victory. As usual with friendlies, both sides made a large number of substitutions and that took some of the pace out of the game.

"Come on boys, let's keep our concentration!" Roy

bellowed from the sidelines as Sweden began to pick up the pace.

But his words were in vain as Zlatan Ibrahimović took control. He scored three more times, including a spectacular overhead kick from 40 yards.

Raheem had been subbed off by then, to give another newcomer a chance to play, so he could only watch helplessly from the bench.

It was amazing to witness such a spectacular goal, but it didn't take the sting out of losing 4-2. Losing never sat well with Raheem.

Raheem was quiet as he shook hands with the Swedes. He'd run at the defence just as he'd been instructed, and he'd been instrumental in making Welbeck's goal, so he knew he'd played well. But all the same it wasn't the kind of first game for his country that he'd wanted.

As they headed back to the dressing room, his Liverpool team-mate Stevie G came over to him.

"So, what did you think?" he asked, nudging Raheem.

Raheem was happy to see the familiar face and

answered honestly. "I hate that we lost, but I loved playing. I can't imagine how mad it would be to play in a real tournament one day."

Stevie smiled. He had a feeling it wouldn't be long before Raheem found out just how mad it was.

9
AT ALL COSTS

April 2014, Anfield Stadium, Liverpool
Liverpool v Man City

Raheem closed his eyes and listened to the noise booming around the stadium and penetrating the walls of the dressing room.

"AND YOU'LL NEVER WALK ALONE ... "

The Liverpool fans hadn't seen a league title come to Anfield in almost 30 years, and now it was really looking quite possible.

It was a far cry from last season, when Liverpool had slumped to a seventh-place finish and missed out on European football.

So far this season, Liverpool had hammered Spurs 5-0, Arsenal 5-1 and Man United 3-0. They were scoring goals at an unprecedented rate and Raheem was at the centre of it, with Brendan opting to play with four up front: Suárez, Daniel Sturridge, Coutinho and Raheem.

This setup gave Jordan Henderson a lot of work to do, but it was brutally effective and it quickly became apparent that the only team that could catch them was Man City.

The very team they were playing today.

"We're on for a record number of points – and they're still right behind us," Raheem complained to Luis as they sat together listening to the fans singing.

"There's only one thing to do, Raheem … win at all costs," replied Luis with a wink.

Raheem scoffed at his little joke. It was what Luis had said last year, when Raheem had asked Luis what he'd been thinking when he'd bitten a Chelsea player. Win at all costs.

But this time Luis was right. They needed to win this match against Man City. *Almost* at all costs, anyway.

Raheem glanced at the other players. He could see that they were feeling the same pressure. He wasn't the only one to pick up on the tension in the room, and Stevie was quick to pull the whole team together.

"Right, boys. I know there are a lot of questions going round about whether we're going to win the title, or whether we're just going to throw it all away."

He spoke with a calm authority and all eyes were fixed on him.

"I only want to say that I believe we will win this title. We all know we can do it. But I also want to say that, as long as every one of us in this room gives everything out on that field, then it doesn't matter whether we come first or twentieth," he continued. "We will have done our best."

It was what the team needed to hear, and they lined up in the tunnel, fired up by his words.

Brendan had stuck to his guns and picked the same team that had got them this far, choosing not to switch to a more defensive system against a better side.

As they walked out on to the pitch, all Raheem could think was how glad he was that he wasn't a Man City player right now. Almost 70,000 fans were united against them and in support of Liverpool. If the Liverpool players hadn't been up for the game before, they certainly were now.

This atmosphere carried Liverpool through the opening five minutes as they outfought, outran and outmanoeuvred the might of Man City. In no time Luis Suárez had the ball and was shrugging off the challenges of two City players, before picking out Raheem.

Raheem now had the ball up inside the box. He twisted right, then left, and then right again, sending Vincent Kompany and Joe Hart to the floor, before curling the ball into the open goal.

GOAL!

He couldn't believe it. They were only six minutes in and he'd handed them the lead. It was crucial.

"What a ball!" he yelled, tackling Luis to the floor.

"Forget the ball, Raheem, what a goal!" Luis yelled back, as they ended up in a tangled mess on the Anfield turf, with several other players bundling in on top of them.

Once they were back on their feet, Liverpool continued pushing hard. City keeper Joe Hart was forced into several saves, before Martin Škrtel crashed home a header from a corner, to put Liverpool into a two-goal lead.

"That's one step closer to the title!" Jordan Henderson roared, as they celebrated.

But Man City came out into the second half with a new lease of life and suddenly it was 2-2. Now the game was up for grabs and City had the momentum – they looked the team more likely to get the winner.

Liverpool needed a spark, a moment of magic from someone.

Then suddenly a hopeful ball into the box was scuffed clear by Vincent Kompany. It fell to the feet of Phillipe Coutinho, who struck it first time, whipping the ball into the bottom corner.

GOAL!

"COUTINHOOOO!" Raheem found himself running the match commentary in his mind. He joined the rest of the team in sprinting after the little Brazilian.

"What a goal!" he screamed into his ear.

The rest of the game passed by in a flash, with the roar of the fans carrying Liverpool through to the final whistle.

At full-time, Stevie G summoned the players into a huddle, refusing to let them off the pitch. Raheem looked at the beaming faces of his team-mates.

"Lads, this does not slip now!" Stevie screamed in his thick Scouse accent, "We go again at Norwich next week, but this does not slip!" he roared.

His passion was infectious, and Raheem had never been more sure that they could do it.

He could practically feel the weight of his first professional football trophy in his hands.

10
WORLD CUP, TAKE ONE

June 2014, The Royal Tulip Hotel, Rio de Janeiro, Brazil

Raheem still felt robbed of the Premier League title. Liverpool had been pipped by Man City on the last day of the season, losing the title by just two points.

This must be how his old neighbours on the estate had felt when their TV had been nicked, thought Raheem – gutted.

He sighed at the thought. His neighbours hadn't

locked their back door and they'd paid the price. Just as he hadn't played well enough in that Chelsea match, and he – and the rest of the team – had paid the price too.

He cringed as Stevie's now infamous slip in the game against Chelsea played out in his mind. Liverpool had gone on to lose that game – and it had probably cost them the Premier League title.

The irony wasn't lost on anyone, after the speech he'd given just before the Man City game.

To Raheem, it still just seemed so wrong that they had a record number of points in the Premier League, but it all added up to nothing. Their season had ended without a trophy.

Raheem couldn't torture himself thinking about it any more, so he abruptly sat up, rubbed his eyes and refocused his mind.

In reality, Raheem couldn't have played that badly, because his Liverpool performances had got him here – back in the England squad for a World Cup tournament.

It was a dream come true, even if it hadn't got off to the smoothest start.

England were in a tough group, with Italy, Uruguay and Costa Rica, and their first game had ended in a disappointing 2-1 defeat to Italy. It felt as if the whole country was furious with them.

"How do you deal with it, Wayne?" Raheem asked Wayne Rooney, a few days after the disastrous match. There were various reports in the media that were highly critical of the team's performance, but particularly of Rooney's.

"What do you mean?" he replied.

"The criticism. It always seems so harsh, so over the top," Raheem said. The article he'd flicked through that morning had been equally harsh about Rooney's private life, although Raheem wasn't clear what that had to do with anything.

"I don't read it," Rooney said, shrugging his shoulders. "I know when I've played well, and I know when I've played badly. Who cares what other people think?"

Raheem nodded, though he didn't think that he'd

be as cool in the same situation. He didn't want his mum reading anything bad about him, even if it was completely made up.

But Raheem had managed to cast aside any worries about potential criticism back home. The secret was to stay focused on the job at hand, and his was the best job in the world: football.

He knew that England could still turn this around.

Their game tomorrow was against Uruguay, who were led by none other than his Liverpool team-mate, Luis. Raheem knew that there were a lot of rumours going around that Luis was injured and wouldn't be able to play, so he thought he'd text him to try to find out the truth:

How's it going, man?

Luis replied in seconds and, as expected, saw through him entirely.

Nice try. You'll have to wait and see.

Luis wasn't only fit, he was in sensational form, and Raheem couldn't help but feel the nerves when he heard the news. He'd always felt bad for the people up against Luis and now he was going to be one of them.

Raheem wasn't the only player who fully appreciated what they were up against. He looked at the other Liverpool players who'd been called up to their team. Glen Johnson was deathly silent and Daniel Sturridge kept his eyes on the floor. They knew as well.

They were right to be worried. Luis scored twice and sent England out of the World Cup.

Raheem was devastated and he knew it would take him a while to come to terms with the fact that his first major tournament with England wasn't going to end with silverware.

First Liverpool, and now England.

At the end of the match, he trudged off the pitch and avoided looking at the fans who had travelled so far to support their national side.

As he walked back to the dressing room, he made a

silent promise to himself. One day he was going to be part of an England side that the fans could be proud of.

II
LIFE WITHOUT LUIS

October 2014, Anfield Stadium, Liverpool
Liverpool v Real Madrid

Everyone could feel the Luis-shaped hole in the team. Suárez had left to join Barcelona, and it hurt, especially for Raheem, who had been looking forward to being reunited with his friend, even if he had single-handedly ended England's World Cup journey.

Brendan Rogers had clearly decided that you couldn't replace Luis with just another player, so instead he'd bought in a fleet, including Rickie Lambert, Adam Lallana, Mario Balotelli and Emre Can.

It was an overwhelming number of new faces.

"How do you want me to play the ball in to you?" Raheem had asked Rickie after one training session. He'd become used to the little passes that he'd done with Luis, but it was clear that Rickie was struggling with them.

"Just try and play it into my feet, or cross it high into the box," Rickie replied. "I'm not the quickest, so there's no point trying to play it in behind."

Raheem was taking this advice on board, but in the next game, against West Ham, it was Mario Balotelli who started up front with him. They'd barely spoken to each other since Balotelli had joined the club, let alone played together, and they struggled to link up. Raheem managed one goal in the game, but Liverpool were ultimately well beaten 3-1.

It wasn't the most inspiring form for the team, especially bearing in mind their forthcoming Champions League game. It was going to be a huge one, against last year's winners: Real Madrid.

Liverpool hadn't been in the Champions League for four years, and all they'd managed so far in the competition was one narrow win and a defeat.

Now they were facing a team fronting the likes of Karim Benzema, Toni Kroos, James Rodríguez and, of course, Cristiano Ronaldo.

Once again, Raheem was starting up front alongside Mario Balotelli. This time, it didn't even matter what their partnership was like — they didn't get the ball at all.

Real Madrid were completely dominant and Cristiano Ronaldo silenced the Anfield crowd with a sensational goal. Raheem could only stand and watch from the other end of the pitch, completely gutted by how their season was going.

By full time Real Madrid had scored twice more to leave Liverpool facing an exit from the Champions League.

"Not much we could do there, boys," Rodgers said at full time. "They've got a lot of world-class players who can do unbelievable things. Sometimes you've just got to hold your hands up and accept that you were outclassed."

Raheem looked fiercely at his manager, who glared back at him, daring him to speak.

Raheem decided to bite his lip.

12
TRANSFER TROUBLE

February 2015, Raheem's home, Liverpool

"It feels like we got lucky last year, mate," Raheem said down the phone. "I think Luis carried us last year, and I just don't think Brendan knows what to do without him."

"It wasn't just Luis and luck last year, Raheem. You played incredibly well," his agent, Aidy Ward, replied. Aidy had watched the twenty-year-old grow increasingly unsettled at Liverpool, and he was concerned about him.

"But I reckon a lot of your team-mates would get what you're saying about Brendan," Aidy continued.

Raheem grunted in agreement. How could they not agree? Liverpool were out of the title race, out of Europe and out of the League Cup. It was all a far cry from the successes of last season.

Raheem hadn't spoken to anyone at Liverpool about this, so he was grateful to be able to talk about it with Aidy.

"You know, Raheem, I've just been talking to Liverpool and they've got a new contract offer for you – a hundred thousand a week. What do you think?"

Raheem hesitated. That was a huge amount of money, but for Raheem the money was neither here nor there. It was the idea of being at Liverpool that he was thinking hard about.

He was young, he was hungry for success and, if he was honest with himself, he wasn't sure how much further Liverpool were going to go as a club under Brendan's leadership.

The thought of still being at Liverpool in a year, two years, or even longer made his stomach do little flips. Was he prepared to wait that long?

"You're not sure, are you?" Aidy said, after a period of silence on the phone. "Don't sweat it. Look, I'm going to tell them we're going to hold off on signing anything until the end of the season. Let's see where it all stands then."

Aidy Ward was an experienced agent. He'd been around long enough to know how tough it was for young lads to leave the club that had given them their first big chance.

"OK. That sounds good," Raheem replied gratefully.

Raheem's phone was buzzing so much it had almost vibrated off the edge of his bedside table when he finally found it. He opened the message from his mum first:

Have you seen this. What's going on?

Confused, he tapped the link his mum had included

in the message. It was a link to a newspaper article, and reading the title felt like a punch to the stomach:

BRENDAN RODGERS: STERLING REJECTS "FANTASTIC OFFER"

As Raheem read on, he felt completely betrayed. The article gave the impression that he was being greedy in not signing the contract, and that the whole thing was just about money.

In reality, that wasn't the case at all. Raheem was already earning more money than he knew what to do with. Of course he wanted to be paid what he was worth, but he'd barely given the financial offer in the contract a second thought.

His feeling of betrayal quickly turned to anger. How dare Brendan make this situation so public? He felt as if he'd been attacked by the manager, and his instinct was to go straight over to him to have it out.

Instead, he took a deep breath to calm himself, just as he would do after someone had badly fouled him in a match.

Confronting Brendan about this wouldn't solve anything. Best to keep his distance and keep his head down.

Raheem opened up the second text:

R U staying? R U going?

It was from Stevie G.

Raheem didn't know what to text back, but he already knew the answer.

13
THE OFFER

July 2015, Liverpool training ground, Liverpool

Fifty million …

The most expensive English player of all time!

As Raheem walked out of the meeting with the Liverpool officials, he struggled to connect the price tag with himself.

But, if he were honest, it wasn't the price tag that had him quite so giddy. It was the name of the team that had made the offer.

Manchester City. Man City had offered 50 million for him, Raheem Sterling.

It was nuts.

He tried to imagine life at Man City, the kinds of players he'd be training with and the new levels to which he could take his football. He thought about the trophies he'd dreamt about as a child – trophies that at Man City would certainly be within his grasp.

The only thing casting a shadow over the whole thing was the backlash he'd probably face.

He thought back to Liverpool's annual awards ceremony at Anfield in May. He'd been voted Young Player of the Season, and it should have been a wonderful night, but as he'd made his way up to collect the award he'd heard some boos echoing around the ground. It was the worst feeling in the world.

"It's only because you haven't signed a new contract," Daniel Sturridge had said, with a sad smile. "They think you just want money. Plus, the club's not doing so well at the moment, and they need someone to blame."

Raheem couldn't even be bothered to protest his

innocence any more. He'd tried to set the record straight in an interview, to put across what had happened as he saw it, but it hadn't worked. But then, he was a football player, not some kind of media pundit. He was most comfortable behind a ball and most *un*comfortable in front of a microphone.

It seemed that everyone thought he was just a money-grabbing kid – and the press were making it so much worse.

If they were to be believed, he was driving round in flash cars and going to parties every other night. Now Raheem had proof that he wasn't as tough as Wayne Rooney – he *cared* that the press were painting a bad picture of him, but he couldn't see a way of stopping it.

With all that fresh in his mind, he couldn't help but wonder if he should just give in and stay at Liverpool. That was what everyone seemed to want.

He dismissed the thought as soon as it entered his head. He was not going to let the press – or anyone else – bully him into doing things their way.

He was not going to be bullied out of this incredible opportunity at Manchester City.

He looked out of the window at the blue sky and smiled. He was about to take a step that would bring him closer to achieving the things he'd dreamt about as a child – and he'd be doing it wearing a sky-blue shirt.

14

A MANCHESTER MAN

October 2015, Etihad Stadium, Manchester
Man City v Bournemouth

Raheem had grown used to having a guaranteed starting spot at Liverpool.

Walking around the Man City training ground had made him very aware that that wasn't the case any more.

One moment he'd brush shoulders with David Silva, the next he was face-to-face with Kevin De Bruyne.

And then Sergio Agüero was calling for them all to come and practise. It felt like a different world.

But despite needing to fight for a place in a side littered with superstars, Raheem actually felt more relaxed than he had in a long time.

The change of club was proving to be everything he'd hoped for, and with the Liverpool contract issues finally behind him, his focus was back on what he loved most – top-quality football.

"What's it like?" he asked his England team-mate, Joe Hart, as they lined up in the tunnel for their match against Bournemouth.

"What's what like?" Joe replied.

"Winning the title," Raheem pressed.

"Ah! I can't explain it, but I don't need to," Joe laughed, "You'll find out soon enough."

Raheem grinned and found his place in the line. His season had already started very well. Playing with Sergio and David reminded him of playing with Luis at Liverpool. He was learning loads from them and they were helping him develop into the force on the pitch he'd always dreamt of becoming.

"There's goals here," Jesús Navas said to him, glancing at the Bournemouth defence and bringing Raheem's thoughts back to the immediate task in hand.

Only minutes later, Navas was proved right. The ball was fizzed across the box by Pablo Zabaleta, and Raheem was lurking on the line to tap it in.

GOAL!

It wasn't the best goal he'd ever scored, but he celebrated it anyway.

"Hey, Raheem, you can't celebrate that, you know. That doesn't count as a goal here at City," Pablo laughed.

Raheem raised his eyebrows at his team-mate, accepting the challenge to deliver something a bit more spectacular.

The goals continued to flow and Wilfried Bony doubled City's advantage, before Glenn Murray pulled a goal back for Bournemouth.

With half an hour gone, Raheem had the ball again. He cut into the box, feinted to shoot once, and then again, before finally pulling the trigger and firing the ball past the Bournemouth keeper.

GOAL!

"That's more like it, Raheem!" Zabaleta yelled, celebrating with him. "You can have that one!"

"You put half their team on the floor. What a goal!" Kevin de Bruyne bellowed, as he charged over to him.

With seconds remaining before half-time, Raheem had an opportunity for his hat-trick. After a scramble in the box, the ball rebounded to him and he drove it back past the keeper, rippling the back of the net.

GOAL!

It was Raheem's first hat-trick. He channelled the rush of adrenaline, punching his fist in the air in front of the thousands of City fans who were going wild, chanting his name.

He'd known deep down that not everyone had hated him, but after feeling so unpopular for so long, this really meant the world to him.

After all, there was no better way of answering his critics than scoring goals.

15
TAKING THE TROPHY

February 2016, Wembley Stadium, London
Man City v Liverpool, League Cup final

Playing against a former club was something Raheem wasn't sure he'd ever get used to.

He talked to some of the other players about their experiences and thoughts, and their responses were rather mixed.

Some seemed to enjoy the opportunity to show off their new skills and thump their old team, whilst others still found going against ex-team-mates odd, and sometimes more than a little uncomfortable.

Now, in the dressing room before the League Cup final against Liverpool, his old team, Raheem still wasn't sure what he felt, other than a burning desire to win his first trophy.

A win here today would get him exactly that, so it wasn't hard for him to focus on the game and put other thoughts aside.

This was the positive attitude that the City coaches had instilled in him since he'd joined the club.

"I'll tell you what it is, Raheem," Gaël Clichy had said to him before a match against Everton.

"What?"

"When I was at Arsenal, we were more worried about losing than we were about winning. We always went into big games looking to not lose."

Raheem nodded slowly.

"Here at City, we look to win. Every time. That's the difference."

Raheem could see and feel that attitude in the dressing room today. He was surrounded by determined, calm faces, as the players went through their individual routines, preparing for the game. This was a team who had been here before and knew how to win trophies.

In addition, many of the players remembered City's 4-1 defeat against Liverpool earlier in the season, and were keen to take revenge.

Out on the pitch, Raheem felt the same shiver of excitement he always got at Wembley. He thought of his younger self, playing football in a park not a mile away from here, pretending he was up for a cup. Now it was for real.

The game was tight and the deadlock was only broken in the second half. Fernandinho was the man who fired City ahead.

It looked as if Man City were going to hold out for the 1-0 win, but with just a few minutes left it was Raheem's old friend Coutinho who struck for Liverpool.

He slammed the ball into the back of the net after a defensive mix-up, and suddenly extra time and penalties loomed.

"We can still do this, lads!" Kompany shouted from the back, spurring on the City players.

In extra time City were dominant, but Liverpool managed to hold on. The scores stayed level.

It should never have got this far, but it had.

Penalties.

Raheem had never been involved in a penalty shoot-out in a final before, and he had a moment of panic. His legs felt like jelly after 120 minutes of football and he wasn't sure he was up to it.

"Please say I don't have to take one," he muttered to himself.

Luckily he wasn't in the first five penalty-takers from the assigned list, so instead he had the equally nerve-wracking job of watching his team-mates step up.

After City keeper Willy Caballero sensationally saved three penalties in a row, it was up to Yaya Touré to secure the win for City. Raheem joined the whole stadium in a collective holding of breath.

Yaya was the only person who wasn't nervous and he rolled it casually into the back of the net.

GOAL!

Half the stadium erupted whilst the other half collapsed in anguish. City were cup winners!

Raheem roared in celebration, then stood and looked at the sky. He needed a second to take it all in.

He looked affectionately around the stadium. It couldn't have felt more right to be getting his first trophy at Wembley.

He felt sympathy for the Liverpool players, but success only came by winning games, and City had proved consistently that they could do that.

Raheem thought about his move to City from Liverpool. At that moment, it felt like the best decision he'd made in his life.

Yaya noticed his team-mate was standing on his own and went over to him.

"You stick with us and it won't be your last," Yaya said, dragging him towards the celebrations.

Raheem joined the team huddle and soaked up the atmosphere. It was an incredible feeling and, with plenty of time left in the season, one he was hungry to experience again – and sooner rather than later.

16
PEP

August 2016, Man City training ground, Manchester

His name had been bouncing around the training ground since February, when his move to City had been announced, and now here he was. Pep.

"I can't wait for him to start, man," Sergio had said when the move was announced, "I mean, look at what he did with Barcelona."

"But we don't have a Messi," De Bruyne replied.

"Nah, but Raheem can do that," Agüero said, gesturing to Raheem, who'd started laughing.

He too had been excited about Pep Guardiola coming to the club. He was simply one of the best managers in the world and Raheem couldn't wait to show him what he could do with a ball.

But since the February announcement, Raheem's confidence had plummeted. The League Cup they'd won against Liverpool had ended up being their only trophy, after Leicester had shocked the world and won the league title.

And then England had been dumped out of the Euros by minnows Iceland. It had been a major embarrassment and the press had had a field day criticising the England players' performance.

As for Raheem, he was gutted that he hadn't been able to deliver for his country yet again.

He'd thought it couldn't get any worse, until the day after he arrived back in the UK, following the Euros.

"Raheem! The video, the house, the sink – all of it!

Just days after you guys got knocked out the Euros! What *were* you thinking? What was going through your mind?" His agent, Aidy Ward, was on the other end of the phone and he was clearly not happy.

Raheem had bought the house for his mum. He'd known his friends had been round, and they'd joked about filming some stuff, including a jewel-encrusted sink he'd had installed. But Raheem hadn't seen any problem with that.

"But it was a present for my mum!" Raheem protested. "It was something I'd said when I was younger. I just wanted to thank her for – "

"The club don't care about that," Aidy cut him off. "The media are having a field day, saying you couldn't care less about your performances for England, because you're so filthy rich.

"It doesn't make you look good, Raheem, and bad press like this is certainly not good for the club. They are *not* happy, I can tell you."

Raheem had been so angry, but he couldn't find the

words to express it. He'd earned this money, it was *his*. Why couldn't *he* decide what he spent it on?

It always seemed to be everyone else's business how he spent the money he earned. Thinking back, articles saying he'd spent too much on a car, or spent too little in a discount shop, were endless.

He thought back to when he was at Liverpool. Even then, the media had been picking apart every little thing he did, even making stuff up …

As soon as he got off the phone to Aidy, he called his mum.

"I don't understand why they keep singling me out, Mum. At Liverpool, I did the same stuff as Steven Gerrard and Jordan Henderson. At City, I do the same stuff as Joe Hart. But I never see any articles about them."

He paused. The thought that had just entered his head had occurred to him before, but he'd never mentioned it to anybody. But if he couldn't say it to his mum, who could he say it to?

"It's because I'm black."

Nadine sighed down the phone. She'd always known that, for all his struggles in school, her son was no fool.

"Just hold your head up high, Raheem, and always do what *you* think is the right thing. And on the pitch – just keep doing what you're doing!" She laughed, to lighten the tension.

This wasn't the first time Raheem had been faced with bad press and, as before, he didn't know what else he could do.

So he took his mum's advice and put on a brave face. Nevertheless, he was worried that this incident would sour his working relationship with Pep, even before he'd met him.

On Pep's first day with the players, Raheem's heart skipped a beat when Pep waved him over. Was he going to get another lecture about how he'd spent his money, about how all this press was bad for the club?

Raheem walked slowly over to his new manager, keeping his eyes on the floor.

"You're going to be my main man this season, OK?" Pep said, straight away.

Raheem looked up and stared at him blankly. That wasn't what he'd been expecting at all.

But before he could give it any more thought, Pep just carried on. He spoke quickly and Raheem had to concentrate to keep up.

"But I want you to change your movement, OK? I want you to come inside from the right and wait at the back post. Then you'll have tap in after tap in, and goal after goal. You get me, Raheem?"

The man's enthusiasm was infectious and Raheem felt all the events of the past few months fade into the background.

It seemed as if Pep was genuinely rooting for him – and already he felt himself wanting to make the manager proud.

As the day went on, Raheem met some of the new faces Pep had brought with him to Man City: Leroy Sané, Nolito, İlkay Gündoğan and John Stones.

The training ground was charged with a new kind of energy – and Raheem was raring to go.

17
ALWAYS LATE

November 2017, Etihad Stadium, Manchester
Man City v Southampton

It was only November and Raheem had already scored 12 goals this season! It was already more than he'd scored in any other season, and many of them had been crucial late goals in the final minutes of a game.

"How do you keep doing it, Raheem?" Agüero asked him. "It's completely insane!"

Raheem didn't know how to reply. He didn't know

the answer himself. "I'm just in the right place at the right time, I guess."

"I never panic when we need a goal now. I just know that Raheem is going to pull something off," Kyle Walker chimed in.

Raheem's late goals had propelled Man City into a record-breaking winning streak and they were several points clear at the top of the table.

He had also formed a deadly trio up front with Leroy Sané and Sergio Agüero. They were referred to as the SAS, and Raheem was loving it.

These successes were a welcome change after a tough season the previous year.

Pep's first season had ended without any trophies, partly as a result of City's struggles defensively, but the players were still completely behind him. His record at Barcelona and Bayern spoke for itself. Clearly he just needed the chance to settle in.

The previous season had also been personally disappointing for Raheem. Before it had ended, Pep had had a quiet word with him.

"I know you're disappointed with how the season's

gone, and you should be," he'd started, "You're a far better player than your performance this season would indicate.

"But you've got to ignore everything the press are saying, ignore everything but me. Have you got that? You're Raheem Sterling and you're my main man, and next season we're going to win it all. OK?"

Those words were still with Raheem as he marched out onto the pitch to take on Southampton.

The SAS triumvirate was one down today – Leroy Sané was missing with an injury – and in the first half it showed. City were struggling to break down the determined Southampton defence.

At half-time, Pep spurred the team on.

"I don't just want to win the title this year. I want to smash all the records out there. Got that? The rest of the season starts *here* and it starts *now*. Now let's get out there and win."

It worked. Kevin de Bruyne's second-half whipped cross missed all his team-mates, as well as all of the

Southampton defenders, before nestling in the back of the net. City were 1-0 up.

Southampton were undeterred and continued to fight their way back into the game, with Sofiane Boufal sweeping the ball into the back of the net 10 minutes before the end.

It looked as if City's winning streak was coming to an end.

"This is your moment, Raheem," Kyle Walker said, coming over and slapping him on the back.

Raheem's new reputation came with a lot of pressure at times like these, but he always kept his cool. He glanced over to Pep, who gave him a reassuring nod from the dugout.

The time ticked on and the clock ran past the 90-minute mark. Five minutes were added on, and one-by-one they were ticking away.

They were now playing in the 95th minute and it all seemed to be over, when the ball came to Raheem on the edge of the box. Instinctively, he whipped the ball with the inside of his right foot and it sped towards the goal.

He didn't even need to watch the ball – he knew as soon it left his foot that it was in.

GOAL!

He turned and sprinted towards the touchline and looked across to Pep, who was punching the air. Then Raheem was jumped on by all the City players on the bench, as well as those on the pitch. They ended up in a pile of bodies on the floor as they celebrated the incredible late goal.

"You've done it again, Raheem!" He heard De Bruyne holler.

The Premier League was now theirs for the taking, and Raheem wasn't planning on wasting the chance to add to his trophy cabinet.

He was playing the best football of his life – he just wanted the next match to come.

18

WORLD CUP, TAKE TWO

July 2018, Otkritie Arena, Russia
England v Columbia

This World Cup was going better than anyone could
have ever hoped.

Even though he was now a Premier League winner,
Raheem had always struggled in the England squad. It
still felt as if half of the fans didn't want him in the team,
but he consistently gave everything he had out on the
pitch.

Under manager Gareth Southgate they were playing with three at the back and so far it had proved very effective.

In their opening game against Tunisia, with only minutes left on the clock, it had looked as if they were heading for a draw, before Harry Kane had flicked his second ball into the net and sealed the game at 2-1.

The next game, against Panama, had gone even better. England had won 6-1, which had confirmed their place in the next round.

The squad had been living and training in a little football bubble, but word had started to get through to them about how, back home, the country was getting completely behind them.

Raheem's previous experiences with England meant that he took these rumours with a pinch of salt. But the players were soon passing round videos from social media showing big screenings of the England games around the UK.

He smiled at the wild celebrations.

It was only when his mum had texted him and told him that all the headlines back home were about World

Cup Fever, that Raheem had started to appreciate the amount of support they were actually getting.

When he looked on social media there was one message that seemed to be everywhere – the Cup was coming home, and this was the England squad that could do it.

A loss to Belgium in their last game meant that today England were facing Colombia in the last 16.

They were spurred on by the support at home, but they knew this was going to be a tough game. Colombia had top players, including James Rodríguez and Falcao.

As Raheem walked out on to the pitch he was desperate to make an impact. He'd only scored twice for his country – and the last goal had been almost two years ago.

He gave 110% during the match, despite Colombia committing foul after foul and constantly time wasting.

"Come on ref!" Raheem shouted, after he felt the latest kick on his ankles, "How can that not be a yellow?"

The ref waved away his protests and the game continued with the same intensity.

"When is he going to give us something?" Dele Alli said to Raheem, with his hand over his mouth.

The whole team felt that the ref was allowing the Colombians to get away with too much, and they were thrilled when VAR eventually intervened to give England a penalty.

Harry Kane duly put it in the net and, as the minutes passed, it looked as if England were going to hang on for the victory.

Raheem was replaced by Jamie Vardy for the last five minutes and he carried on watching the game nervously from the bench.

Then suddenly, three minutes into injury time, Colombia's Yerry Mina rose to pile home a header and snatch a last-minute equaliser.

Raheem collapsed on the bench with his head on his hands.

The game went to extra time, and then a penalty shootout. Penalty shootouts had always been England's downfall in previous tournaments – it had become a running joke amongst England fans. But this time, could they break with tradition and get a result?

The first person to miss was Jordan Henderson. Advantage Colombia. But then Jordan Pickford pulled off a miracle. It all came down to Eric Dier.

"Have you ever seen him take a penalty?" Raheem asked, turning to Dele on the bench next to him.

"He scores every one he takes in training," Dele said with a shrug.

Dier stepped up. The whole stadium held its breath. A whole country held its breath.

GOAL! 4-3 on penalties!

England had won a World Cup penalty shootout for the first time ever – and were into the quarter finals!

Raheem was overjoyed that their journey wasn't over yet, and he ran out and hugged his team.

The players were on the pitch, singing Southgate's song, along with the fans.

"SOUTHGATE YOU'RE THE ONE ... "

Raheem knew that surviving this test of nerve was the massive lift the team needed.

Sure enough, the next game, against Sweden, was a

much less stressful affair, and they ran out comfortable 2-0 winners.

Next up were Croatia. This semi-final would be the toughest game England had played so far.

It got off to a sensational start with Kieran Trippier putting England ahead after just five minutes, but Croatia were a very good side. They forced their way back into the game with a goal from Ivan Perišić, before Mandžukić struck a winner in extra time.

Croatia were through and England were out.

Raheem, once again, watched from the subs' bench, having been taken off. He was desperately frustrated that he hadn't got a goal, and now his dreams – along with those of the rest of the England team – were over.

"We could have won this, man," he said to Dele alongside him, completely crushed.

"Four years," Dele said soothingly. "We're a young squad. We'll still be in our prime next time around."

Dele had a point, and it gave Raheem a bit more perspective. He'd managed to do one of the things he'd promised himself he'd do, all those years ago at the last World Cup.

He was part of an England squad that had won back the nation's support, and he was proud of that. But he knew what had to come next. He had to score goals.

He turned to Dele and looked him straight in the eye. "Next time, we're bringing it home."

19
STERLING'S STAND

December 2018, Stamford Bridge, London, England
Man City v Chelsea

Back with Man City, Raheem had picked up where he'd left off, putting the disappointment of the World Cup behind him.

The sporadic criticisms of his performance no longer affected him in the same way and, with his help, Man City were now top of the league.

Unlike the previous year, however, they weren't

running away with it. Liverpool were right on their tail, and for every game that City won, Liverpool won one too.

"They just won't go away, will they?" Sergio had said to Raheem in training before their next game. City were away to Chelsea, and needed a win to keep the distance between themselves and Liverpool.

"Raheem, you still know a few Liverpool players. Why don't you try and get inside their heads?" Kyle joked.

"I don't think they'd take a phone call from me," Raheem replied.

Come match day at Stamford Bridge, Raheem was using everything he'd worked on in training to try to make an impact.

As usual, his mind was so focused on the game that the shouts of the crowd had receded into a distant roar. But as he went to grab the ball for a corner kick, his focus was broken. He tuned in to the words of one fan that he could hear.

They were comments about the colour of his skin.

Like all players, Raheem had experienced routine abuse at football grounds for as long as he could remember. But this was different. Worse, he was stunned by how *incensed* this man appeared to be.

So stunned, in fact, that all he could do was let out a little laugh.

Some of his team-mates exchanged puzzled looks, not sure what Raheem was finding so funny.

The game continued, with Chelsea eventually running out 2-0 winners.

But while the rest of the City team concerned themselves with the fact that their winning streak had come to an end, Raheem was reflecting on what he'd heard from the crowd.

What *could* have made this 'fan' so angry? Raheem found himself revisiting that conversation he'd had with his mum when the press had been targeting him. It had been a long time ago, but he knew it had never been more relevant.

Back then, he hadn't known what to do about it, but now it seemed so simple. He knew he had to speak up. He owed it to himself as well as to other people of colour.

By the time he was back in Manchester, he had tapped out a message that he wanted to share with the world, and he'd even found an example to back up what he was saying. Without consulting anyone, he hit 'Send' and put down his phone.

The response that followed from the football world – and from the mainstream press – was incredible.

So often it had seemed as if everyone was against Raheem, but now it felt quite the opposite. The press *did* need to change the way they were presenting black players like Raheem. It *was* unfair and it *was* fuelling racism, as well as tarnishing their beloved sport.

Raheem felt as if he'd won a battle, one he hadn't realised he'd been fighting for so long.

As he read through the messages of support that had come streaming in, he felt empowered. Yes, he'd been right all along.

He directed that feeling towards the coming season. The whole team were in exceptional form and he could think of no reason why they couldn't bring home, not one, not two, but three trophies.

That would give the media something to write about.

20
SAME PERSON

August 2019, Wembley Arena, London
Man City v Liverpool

They were the big new rivals in football, and now they were competing in the FA Community Shield.

Manchester City and Liverpool.

"We've got this lads. I mean, they're only here because we can't play against ourselves!" Bernardo grinned at the other City players.

He was right. This annual match was always between

the previous season's winners of the Premier League and the FA Cup winners. Last season, City had won both, together with the League Cup, so Liverpool had been called in, as the runners up, to face them.

For Raheem, the meeting of these two clubs still gave him strange feelings, forcing him to look back on his career so far.

Liverpool had given him his first big chance, at the age of fifteen, and he had many great memories of playing in the red shirt.

Even though some bad moments had followed, he still treasured those times with Luis and the other lads.

And now he was standing with his current team, the team that had given him a new lease of life and made him into the player he was today.

True to the drama of the occasion, the match went to penalties.

Liverpool were first up to take a penalty, and Xherdan Shaqiri was the man. He was up against

Claudio Bravo in the City goal, who looked huge against the backdrop of the net. It didn't matter. Shaqiri scored.

İlkay Gündoğan was up for City.

"Germans don't miss pens," Kyle muttered to Raheem, who laughed quietly back at him. He was right and İlkay slotted it away easily, sending the Liverpool keeper the wrong way.

Gini Wijnaldum was up next for Liverpool. It was a short run up and, even from far away, Raheem could see that he looked a little edgy.

Claudio threw himself to his right and met the ball with a strong palm. It flew away from the goal and towards the right-hand touchline.

Advantage City!

The next few penalties went by in a flash. Bernardo Silva scored for City, then Lallana pulled one back.

Foden scored, then Oxlade-Chamberlain levelled it up.

"Is anyone else going to miss?" Raheem murmured to Kyle next to him.

"You not taking one, Raheem?" he asked.

"My legs are gone, mate," Raheem replied, shaking his head.

He was already quietly satisfied with the early goal he'd scored in the game. Even though the two teams had met many times before, that had been Raheem's first against his former team.

Zinchenko was up next for City, and he put his penalty away, despite Liverpool keeper Alisson getting a big hand to it.

Then Mohamed Salah scored for Liverpool, meaning that the pressure was on Gabriel Jesus to win it for City.

"Go on, Gabi, you've got this," Raheem muttered, more to himself than to anyone else, before holding his breath.

GOAL!

City had done it – they'd won the Community Shield! It was yet another trophy for Raheem to add to his collection.

His record now stood at two Premier League trophies, one FA Cup trophy, three League Cup trophies and two Community Shields.

Raheem rarely stopped and added it all up like that, but when he did, he couldn't help but be a little dazed.

He'd achieved so much with his current, record-breaking team, as well as with his national side.

Only a few months back, he'd scored a hat-trick for England in a 5-0 win over the Czech Republic, in a Euro 2020 qualifier. His goal drought for the national team seemed to be well and truly over and, for him, the Euros couldn't come soon enough.

As he celebrated today's win with City, he thought back to all the hat-tricks and goals in his career. He was pleased still to be able to remember his first one, against Reading, just as Stevie G had said he would.

When the celebrations started to subside, Raheem looked around the familiar arena.

No matter how many times he played at Wembley, it still made him think of himself as a young kid, playing football down the road and looking longingly to where he was standing right now.

He knew that that young kid would be proud. Proud that he'd not let anything break his spirit or change him.

He was in so many was the same person he'd been then – one who just loved football and wanted to push himself to be the best he could possibly be.

And he wasn't done yet.

HOW MANY
HAVE YOU READ?

Printed in the USA
CPSIA information can be obtained
at www.ICGtesting.com
JSHW022315291223
54568JS00002B/22

9 781948 585903